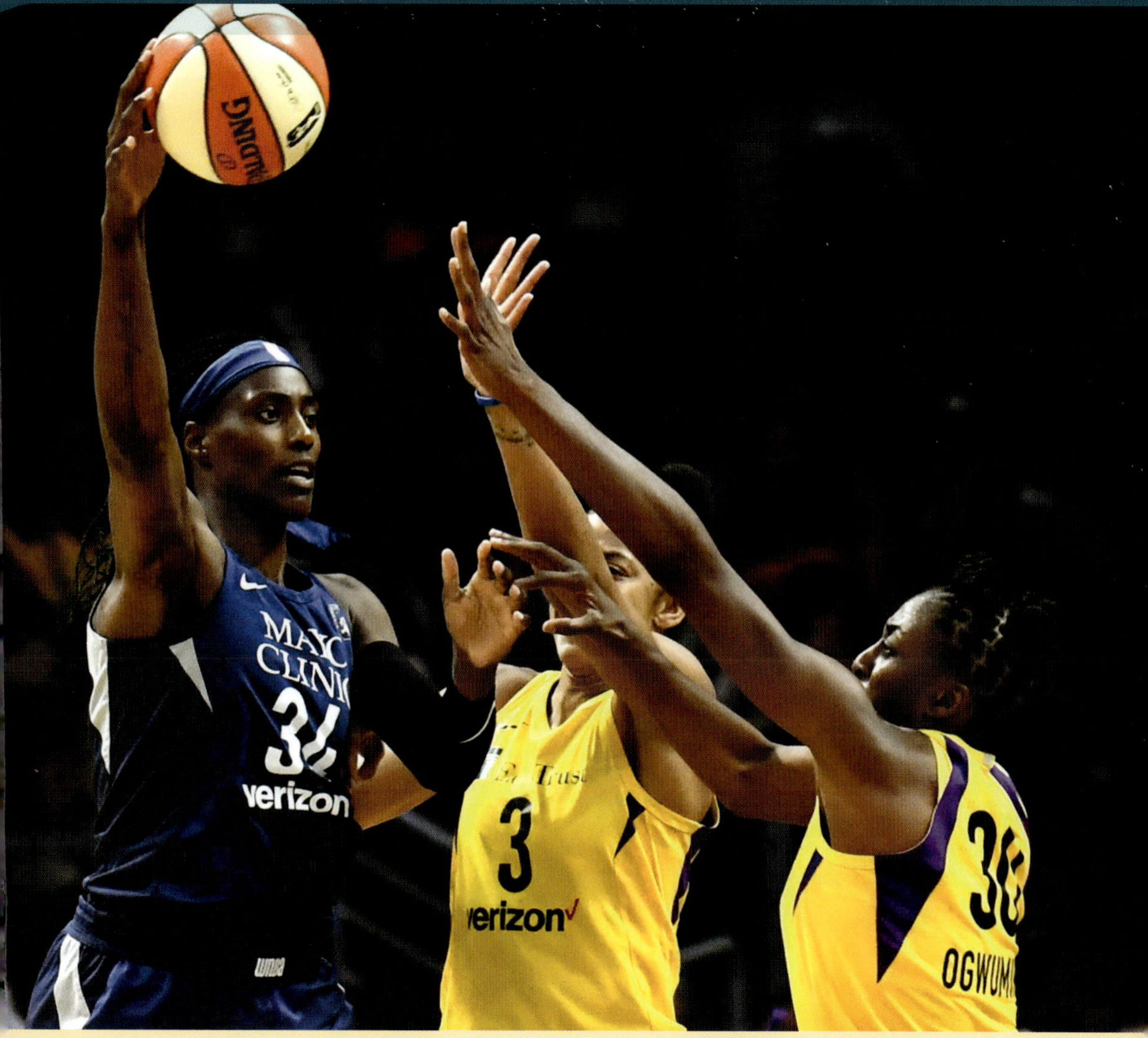

WHAT IT TAKES TO BE A PRO
BASKETBALL PLAYER

by Joanne Mattern

www.12StoryLibrary.com

Copyright © 2020 by 12-Story Library, Mankato, MN 56002. All rights reserved. No part of this book may be reproduced or utilized in any form or by any means without written permission from the publisher.

12-Story Library is an imprint of Bookstaves.

Photographs ©: Keith Birmingham/Associated Press, cover, 1; pio3/Shutterstock.com, 4; zhangjin_net/Shutterstock.com, 5; Bukharev Oleg/Shutterstock.com, 6; space_heater/Shutterstock.com, 6; Natursports/Shutterstock.com, 7; PD, 8; Vladapreda/CC4.0, 9; PD, 10; Lorie Shaull/CC4.0, 11; Gage Skidmore/CC3.0, 11; salajean/Shutterstock.com, 12; Rawpixel.com/Shutterstock.com, 13; Aspen Photo/Shutterstock.com, 14; Aspen Photo/Shutterstock.com, 15; Ikrill/Shutterstock.com, 15; Zennie Abraham/CC2.0, 16; Keith Allison/CC2.0, 17; A_Lesik/Shutterstock.com, 18; Dmitry Argunov/Shutterstock.com, 19; Ginnyyj/Shutterstock.com, 20; Keith Allison/CC2.0, 21; Tumar/Shutterstock.com, 21; Gerald Herbert/Associated Press, 22; Massachusetts Office Of Travel & Tourism/CC2.0, 23; Craig Lassig/Associated Press, 24; Keith Allison/CC2.0, 25; Richard W. Rodriguez/CC2.0, 26; Australian Paralympic Committee/CC3.0, 27; Michele Morrone/Shutterstock.com, 28; TonyTheTiger/CC4.0, 29

ISBN
9781632357601 (hardcover)
9781632358691 (paperback)
9781645820437 (ebook)

Library of Congress Control Number: 2019938633

Printed in the United States of America
July 2019

About the Cover
Minnesota Lynx center Sylvia Fowles (34) makes a pass at the WNBA playoffs in 2018.

Access free, up-to-date content on this topic plus a full digital version of this book. Scan the QR code on page 31 or use your school's login at 12StoryLibrary.com.

Table of Contents

Life as a Basketball Pro: The Real Story 4

A Day in the Life 6

A Brief History of the Game 8

Women Are Welcome 10

Starting Young 12

Making It to the Top 14

It's Not Just about the Shots 16

Overseas Ball 18

Staying in Shape 20

The Best of the Best 22

After the Buzzer 24

Giving Back 26

Fun Facts about Basketball 28

Glossary 30

Read More 31

Index 32

About the Author 32

Life as a Basketball Pro: The Real Story

Swish! There are few moments in sports more exciting than a basketball falling through the net to score a goal. Maybe playing professional basketball is your dream. It seems like it would be wonderful to play pro basketball or be an NBA star.

It's fun to play a sport and get paid very well for it. But being a professional basketball player is also a tough job. Only a few are lucky enough to make it to the top, and they work hard to stay there.

NBA players are among the most fit and talented athletes on the planet. To stay that way, players exercise every day. They can't even sleep late, often getting up by 7 a.m. They shoot baskets with their teammates in the morning. If there is a game that night, players usually watch films of the team they are going to face. Even during the off-season, players practice their

Practice starts early each day.

Pro basketball player Chang Lin lifts weights to get ready for each season.

basketball skills and work out with weights to stay in shape.

Travel is another difficult part of an NBA player's life. Pro players have games all over the country. They spend lots of time away from their families and friends. Staying in different hotels in strange cities can become no fun after a while.

Still, playing professional ball can be a cool way to make a living.

48
Minutes of actual playing time during an NBA game

- Games usually last about 2 hours and 15 minutes.
- Players often sneak candy, popcorn, or coffee while they are sitting on the bench.
- Players usually sit in the same seats courtside. The biggest stars get the best seats.

A Day in the Life

For an NBA player, there is a lot to do almost every day. During the season, he probably wakes up early in the morning. He eats a big breakfast, which might include eggs, hash browns, and toast. He might go on the internet, make phone calls, or read a newspaper. Then it's time to get to work.

If players are at home and not on the road, they usually arrive at the courts between 10 and 11 in the morning. They work out for about two hours. After a break for lunch, they may relax in a hot tub or do more workouts with weights. Some players like to study videos of famous basketball stars. They try to figure out how to add the stars' successful moves to their own style of playing.

After lunch, they take a nap. If there is a game that night, players return to the arena and get ready. They may see the athletic trainer to treat any injuries and make sure their bodies are fit. They put on their uniforms, talk to the coach, and listen to some music to get pumped up. Then they hit the court.

After the game, players might talk to the media. Others might lift weights or go out to eat before heading home to bed.

82
Number of games in an NBA season

- Teams play about three games per week.
- The regular season lasts six months, from mid-October to mid-April.
- The best teams go on to the playoffs. These last from April to the NBA Finals in June.

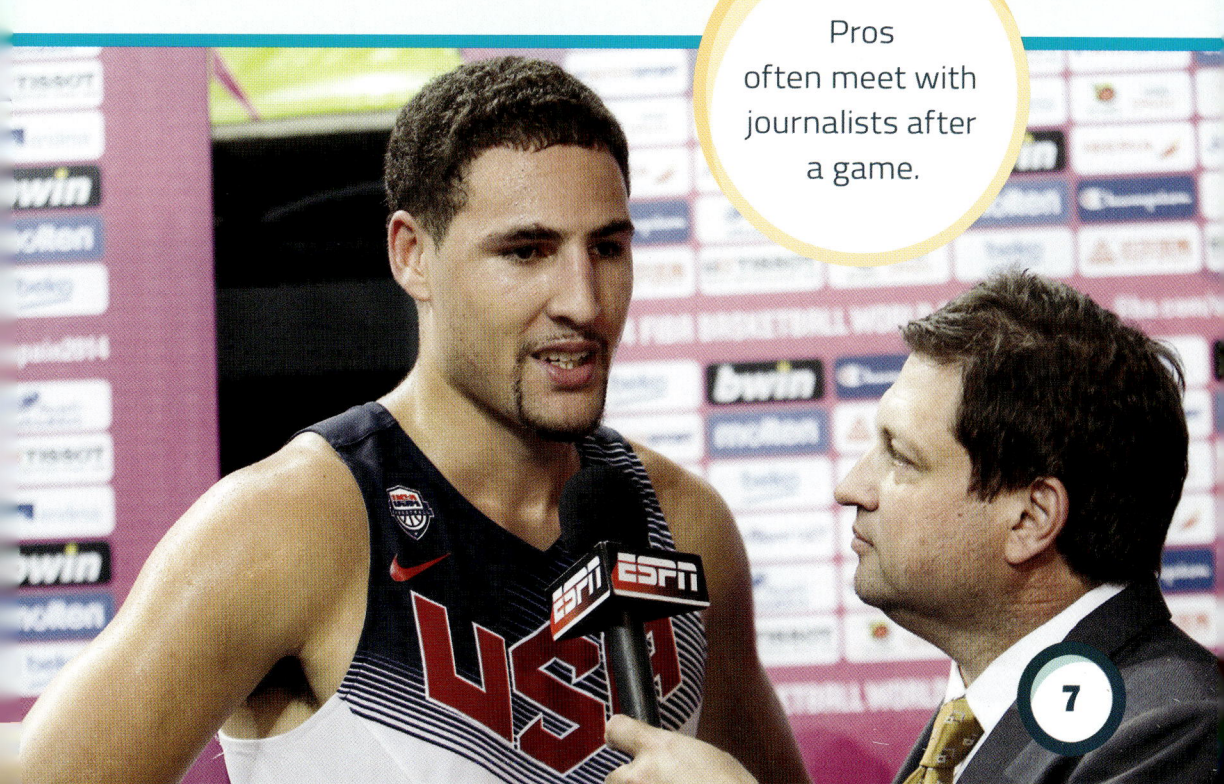

Pros often meet with journalists after a game.

A Brief History of the Game

While most sports have been played for centuries, basketball is relatively new. It was invented in America fewer than 130 years ago. In December 1891, James Naismith was a college gym teacher in Springfield, Massachusetts. He needed a game his students could play inside. Instead of playing fun outdoor games like football, they were stuck doing marching drills and exercises.

Naismith came up with the idea of throwing a ball at a target. He nailed two peach baskets to balcony rails and wrote 13 rules for a new game. He called it "basketball."

Naismith's game spread around the nation. Professional leagues formed by the 1920s. In 1949, two leagues got together and formed the National Basketball Association (NBA).

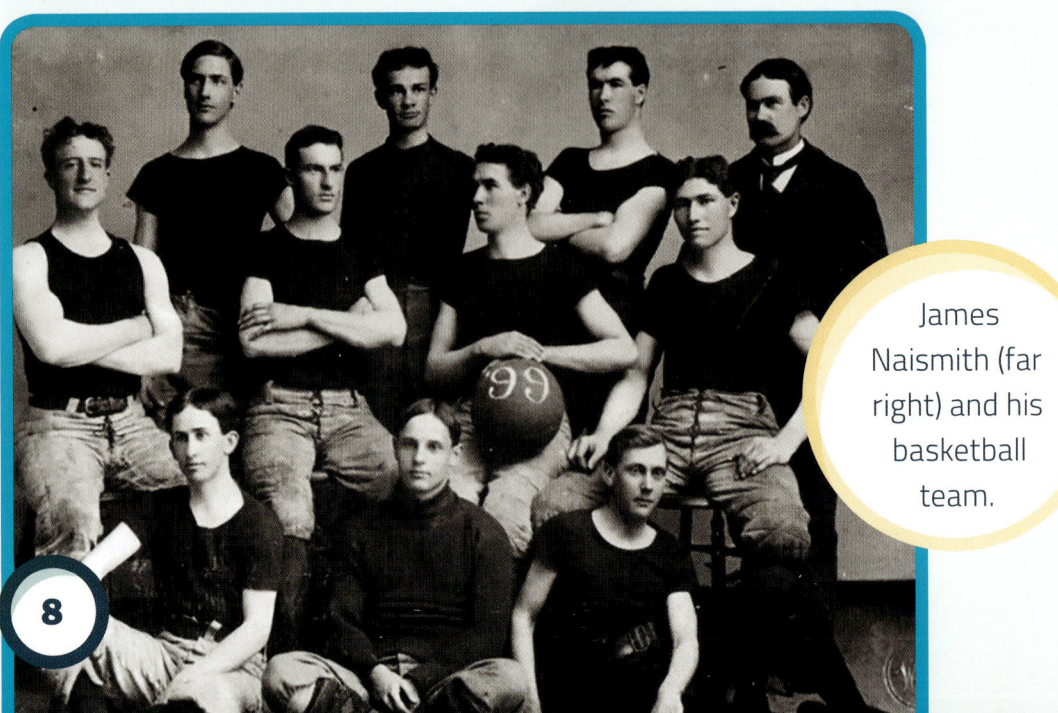

James Naismith (far right) and his basketball team.

Kareem Abdul-Jabbar making his Skyhook shot.

Over the years, basketball and its rules have changed a lot. Originally, a goal was worth one point. In 1896, this changed to two points. In 1977, the NBA adopted a three-point shot. Dribbling was not allowed until 1901. In 1954, the NBA introduced the 24-second shot clock to speed up the game.

1936
Year when basketball became an Olympic sport

- James Naismith tossed the ball up for the first Olympic tip-off. He also presented the medals at the end of the game.
- That year, 21 teams played.
- The United States beat Canada 19-8.

PLAYERS WHO CHANGED THE RULES

Some basketball players are so good they force changes in the rules of the game. At one time, the foul lane was 12 feet (3.6 m) wide. This wasn't enough to stop Wilt Chamberlain from scoring anytime he was near the basket. In 1964, the NBA widened the lane to 16 feet (4.9 m). Between 1967 and 1977, dunking was outlawed in college basketball to stop Lew Alcindor from scoring so often. So Alcindor, later known as Kareem Abdul-Jabbar, invented a shot called the Skyhook.

4

Women Are Welcome

Most professional sports do not have leagues for women. Basketball is different. Professional leagues for women have been around since the 1990s.

The first women's basketball team was organized at Smith College in Massachusetts in 1893. This was shortly after James Naismith invented the game. For the next 100 years, girls played basketball on college and other school teams. Women's basketball was an exhibition sport in the Olympics in the 1920s. In 1976, it became a regular Olympic sport.

In 1978, the Women's Basketball League (WBL) was formed, but it

The Smith College 1902 women's basketball team.

$50,000
Annual starting salary for a WNBA player

- The annual starting salary for an NBA player is over $580,000.
- The highest WNBA salary is $110,000 per year.
- Many WNBA players can earn more money playing in Europe than the United States.

Angel McCoughtry (35) of the Atlanta Dream in 2018.

only lasted for three years. Finally, in 1996, the NBA began a women's league called the WNBA.

The WNBA started with eight teams. Each was located in a city that already had an NBA team.

The league added more teams in the years that followed. The WNBA rules are a bit different than the NBA rules, and the ball is one inch smaller than the NBA ball. However, the action is just as exciting.

MIGHTY ANN MEYERS

Ann Meyers is one of the greatest female basketball players in history. She grew up playing basketball with her brother and his friends. In 1976, she joined the first US Olympic women's basketball team. But her biggest moment came in 1979, when she became the first woman signed to an NBA team. The Indiana Pacers signed her, but she never made it past training camp. Meyers was inducted into the National Basketball Hall of Fame in 1993.

5

Starting Young

Pro basketball players usually start playing as kids.

Most pro basketball players start playing when they are just kids. Children can begin learning the basics of bouncing, throwing, and catching the ball when they are five or six years old. When they are seven to nine years old, it's time to join a youth team.

There are several youth leagues for young players. One of the most common is the Catholic Youth Organization, or CYO.

14
Percentage of children ages 6 to 12 who played youth basketball in 2017

- More than 4 million children played youth basketball that year.
- Most child athletes play two sports.
- Basketball is the most popular youth sport in America.

These leagues are run by volunteers in Catholic parishes, but you do not have to be Catholic to play. Many other churches, local organizations, and communities also run youth basketball leagues.

Professional basketball players often have happy memories about playing for church or youth leagues. Point guard Jrue Holiday says his favorite basketball moments did not happen in the NBA. He recalls great times playing with his brother in a local church league when he was young. Back then, he played just for the joy of playing.

When children reach middle school and high school, they can usually play on school teams. Another way to play is to join the AAU, or Amateur Athletic Union. This organization has been around since 1888. Boys and girls as young as seven years old can join the AAU. Players can play on AAU teams until they turn 19. The AAU sponsors local, state, and national competitions.

THINK ABOUT IT

What is your favorite memory of playing a sport? What made that moment special to you?

6

Making It to the Top

Another plus to playing on your high school team comes later. Most college players are recruited from high schools. College coaches hear about great players. Players can also send coaches videos of themselves playing. Getting a spot on a good college team is the best way to move on to the NBA.

Each year, the NBA recruits college players through a draft held in June. College players usually declare they want to be part of the draft after the NCAA championships. Then they train hard for several months.

College coaches often recruit great high school players.

There are several ways to go from playing for your local team to being a pro in the NBA or WNBA. Most players start their pro careers by playing for their high school teams. Playing for your high school team might be the first time you have to try out and be good enough to earn a place.

If a player is lucky enough to be picked during the draft, he probably won't join the NBA team right away. Instead, players usually start in the G League. This is the minor league of the NBA. Players in G League learn important skills while they play against other G League teams. This is a great way for a player to show the big shots that he is ready for the big leagues.

60
Number of players in the NBA draft

- The odds of playing high school basketball are 1 in 36.
- The odds of playing college ball are 1 in 50.
- The odds of making it to the NBA are 3 in 10,000.

MARCH MADNESS

Held in March, the NCAA Tournament is one of the major sports events of the year. Sixty-eight college teams qualify for the tournament. They play in rounds until the final showdown between two teams. Every year, there are surprising upsets and games. The favorite team might be eliminated early, or that team might win it all.

7

It's Not Just about the Shots

Michael Jordan and Kobe Bryant—two of the NBA's best players.

Many people think the best players are the ones who score lots of points. But there is a lot more to being successful in the NBA or WNBA than making baskets. Michael Jordan says that a player could have all the physical ability in the world, but it wouldn't matter if he didn't learn the basics of the game. Jordan also says that talent can win games, but teamwork and intelligence win championships.

To succeed in the pros, players must be well-rounded. They need to be great at passing the ball and making assists. Former point guard and current head coach Jason Kidd says that passing is about anticipation. Hand-eye coordination is important, too.

16

82
Number of games LeBron James played during the 2018 season

- This is the number of games in an NBA season. So James played every game.
- James is always aware of where other players on his team are, and how to get the ball from one to another.
- James is also a team leader who knows the strengths and weaknesses of everyone on his team.

Professional basketball players also need excellent defensive skills. A team doesn't just need to score. It needs to keep the other team from scoring. Defensive skills come from teamwork. Everyone on the team has a part to play in keeping the ball out of the other team's hands.

The best players are also strong and speedy. They have a lot of stamina. It's hard work running up and down the court for hours. Top players like Kobe Bryant spend hours in the gym so they can be their best on the court.

Kobe Bryant practices almost every day to be his best.

THINK ABOUT IT
Is there a sport you're good at or really enjoy? What are the basics you had to learn at the start?

8

Overseas Ball

The NBA and the WNBA are not the only games in town. There are many teams in other countries where an American baller can make his or her mark and get paid to play.

Playing basketball overseas can be a lot of fun. The teams are well-known and have lots of fans. Players are celebrities. If you like the idea of being asked for autographs, playing in Europe, Asia, or South America could be just the ticket.

International players get to travel widely. They visit many beautiful cities they might never have the chance to see. They meet interesting people from all over the world. Many players make new friends for life.

International players get paid reasonably well. Players can earn between $1,500 and $20,000 per month. A player's salary depends on what team he or she plays for, how good his or her skills are, and other factors.

Of course, playing overseas isn't all wonderful. Players get homesick. It's not easy to deal with another

Overseas pro basketball players have a lot of fans.

language, new customs, and unfamiliar food. Even the game and the training are different than they are in the United States. Still, playing overseas can be a great adventure and a great way to make your basketball dreams come true.

8 months
Length of a foreign basketball season

- The schedule runs from September to May.
- Most teams play one game a week.
- Italy, Spain, France, and Russia have the most competitive teams.

FROM START TO FINISH

Some NBA players start their careers overseas. Others finish there. In 2016, Amar'e Stoudemire retired from the NBA. The power forward and center had played in the NBA for 14 years. But his basketball days weren't over. Instead, he signed on with Hapoel Jerusalem Basketball Club. During the 2018–2019 season, Stoudemire averaged just over 10 points a game.

9

Staying in Shape

Running up and down the court, shooting baskets, and dodging other players can be physically demanding. NBA players work out every day to keep their bodies in top shape from head to toe.

Players go through a series of exercises. These include sprinting, pull-ups, and squats. They also lift weights to strengthen their bodies. They run to improve their stamina and agility.

Players also work on building mental toughness. Someone who is mentally tough has a lot of determination. He or she keeps trying to achieve a goal, even if that goal is hard to reach.

Mentally tough players do not accept no for an answer. When problems come up, players face them head on and look for help if they need it.

Staying positive is also important. Instead of thinking, "I hate running,"

Players who practice running improve their physical and mental stamina.

> Fitness is critical to Lebron James playing well.

$1.5 million
What LeBron James spends on fitness every year

- James has a team of scientists, coaches, and trainers who work with him to design top training routines.
- He has a full gym, a hot tub, and an ice tub in his home.
- Teammates have said that James sees his body as an investment in his future.

a player can fill his or her head with thoughts like, "Running will make me strong." Positive thinking is a powerful tool.

GETTING HURT ON THE COURT

Like any athletes, basketball players can get hurt. The most common injuries are sprains and bruises to their feet, ankles, knees, and hips. Players can also damage their hands and wrists. Injuries to the mouth and teeth happen a lot, too. That's because it's easy to take an elbow to the mouth or get hit in the face by the ball.

10

The Best of the Best

NBA and WNBA players have many ways to shine. The best of the best can be named All-Stars, MVPs, and more.

The NBA All-Star Game is the high point of All-Star Weekend, which takes place every February. Events include the Slam Dunk Contest, the Three-Point Contest, and the Rising Stars Challenge. The best players compete against each other in the All-Star Game.

The WNBA hosts an All-Star Game in July. The first game was played at New York City's Madison Square Garden in 1999.

The NBA used to announce its Most Valuable Players, or MVPs, in early May. In 2017, they changed the date to late June, after the season ends. Awards are voted on by the media. Until 2017, broadcasters working for the teams could vote. But that changed, too. Now only independent media can vote on the awards.

For the very best players, their basketball road ends at the Naismith Memorial Basketball Hall of Fame. The Hall of Fame is in Springfield, Massachusetts, where basketball began. Players must be retired from the NBA

Derrick Jones Jr., of the Phoenix Suns, competes in the Slam Dunk Contest in 2017.

22

for four years before they are eligible for the Hall. Special committees choose players to be considered for induction. An Honors Committee decides who will be inducted.

The Women's Basketball Hall of Fame opened in Knoxville, Tennessee, in 1999.

THINK ABOUT IT

Women have been inducted into the Naismith Hall of Fame. Men have been inducted into the Women's Hall of Fame. Find a few examples of each and share the reasons why.

1959
Year when the Naismith Memorial Basketball Hall of Fame began

- As of 2019, there are about 300 members in the Hall.
- There have been three Hall of Fame buildings. The latest opened in 2002.
- The museum contains about 40,000 square feet (3,716 sq m) of basketball exhibits and history.

11

After the Buzzer

Professional basketball players make great money. However, their careers are usually short. The average NBA career lasts less than five years. Although NBA and WNBA players can play overseas or in other pro leagues, they will probably retire from the sport by the time they are in their late thirties. What can they do for the rest of their lives? There are many answers.

Kobe Bryant retired from the NBA at age 37. He believes that finding a new passion is the key to a happy life after basketball. Bryant's passion is investing money in new tech companies so they can grow. Managing his investments is Bryant's new job.

Many players stay in the basketball world. They may become coaches. Others, like Charles Barkley, Shaquille

Shaquille O'Neal (left) and Charles Barkley have both made their mark in broadcasting since retiring from playing.

O'Neal, and Chris Webber make their mark in broadcasting. Talking about basketball is fun when you know the game inside and out.

Others take a different route. After playing in the NBA and on various international teams, Maceo Baston opened a cupcake store. Hall of Famer Karl Malone bought into many businesses, including a tree farm, a restaurant, and a clothing store. Charlie Ward, who was a star football player in college before playing in the NBA, became a high-school football coach. And Adrian Dantley, a Hall of Famer who scored over 23,000 points during a 15-year career, now works as a crossing guard. Why? Because Dantley enjoys being around children and doesn't want to sit around the house all day.

$24.7 million
What the average NBA player earns during his career

- NBA players have the highest average career salary of all pro sports.
- Kevin Garnett earned more than $300 million during his 19-year career.
- Many players earn less than the average because their careers are short.

Kobe Bryant went into investing after he retired from basketball.

12

Giving Back

Many basketball stars are stars off the field, too. They take part in charity events while they are playing and after they retire. NBA players have a lot of money and the opportunity to help others. It's a win-win for all.

Many NBA stars focus on education and academic success. Through his family foundation, LeBron James is helping students in his hometown of Akron, Ohio. The foundation provides "I Promise" scholarships to students at the University of Akron. In 2018, James opened an "I Promise" charter school for low-income, low-achieving students.

In 2012, Russell Westbrook started the Why Not? Foundation. It supports community-based education and family service programs. It encourages children to believe in themselves. The Miami Heat's Dwyane Wade launched the Wade's World Foundation. It supports community-based organizations that promote education, health, and social skills for kids at risk. Wade

NBA player Grant Hill coaches Special Olympics athletes at a basketball camp.

26

4.7 million
Hours of service given by NBA Cares

- Begun in 2005, NBA Cares is the league's social responsibility program.
- It supports education, youth, and family development in 37 countries around the world.
- Players and staff give time and money to organizations like Special Olympics, Boys and Girls Clubs, UNICEF, and the Make-A-Wish Foundation.

says he wants his life to be bigger than basketball.

All-Star Stephen Curry travels around the world for many health, human and animal rights, and environmental causes. He has worked with the Animal Rescue Foundation and the United Nations. He is helping the Nothing But Nets campaign to stop the spread of malaria. Millions of people each year get sick with this life-threatening disease.

WOMEN CARE, TOO

WNBA Cares is part of NBA Cares. WNBA Cares encourages young people to be fit and active. It works to educate women about breast cancer. It runs a Read to Achieve program to encourage families to read together.

Fun Facts about Basketball

- Until 1929, basketball was played with a soccer ball.

- The average NBA player can jump about 28 inches (71 cm) off the ground.

- The highest-scoring game in NBA history took place on December 13, 1983. The Detroit Pistons beat the Denver Nuggets 186-184 in a game with three overtimes.

- Wilt Chamberlain is the only NBA player to score 100 points in a game. He led the Philadelphia Warriors to a 169-147 win over the New York Knicks on March 2, 1962.

- Sheryl Swoopes was the first player signed to the WNBA. She was also the first WNBA player to have a shoe named after her—Nike's Air Swoopes.

The highest NBA vertical jump record is 48 inches (1.2 m).

- In November 1979, Philadelphia 76er Darryl Dawkins shattered the backboard when he dunked the basketball in a game against the Kansas City Kings. Less than a month later, he did it again against the San Antonio Spurs. The second time, Dawkins also yanked down the metal rim.

- In an NBA game, each team gets six time-outs. They have to use at least four, whether they want to or not.

- In the past, a basketball team could have six players on the court, but only if the referees did not notice the extra man. Once they noticed, the sixth man had to leave, but any points the team scored stayed on the board.

- NBA players have just 10 seconds to make a free throw. Karl Malone took so long to make free throws that the crowd would count to 10 while they waited for him to shoot.

- It is against the rules for a player to punch the ball with his fist.

Sheryl Swoopes in 2014.

Glossary

agility
The ability to move quickly and easily.

broadcasting
Transmitting a program on radio or TV.

draft
In sports, a process professional teams use to choose new players.

dribble
In basketball, to bounce the ball while walking or running down the court.

exhibition sport
In the Olympics, an unofficial sport. It is not eligible for medals.

foundation
An organization that gives money to charity.

induct
Admit someone to an organization.

invest
Provide money to someone to start a business.

league
A group of sports clubs.

media
People who report, broadcast, and publish the news. Also the TV stations, newspapers, news magazines, and radio stations that communicate the news to the public.

recruit
Ask someone to join a team or organization.

scholarship
Money paid to support a student's education.

stamina
The ability to continue physical effort.

Read More

Doeden, Matt. *The NBA Playoffs: In Pursuit of Basketball Glory*. Minneapolis, MN: Millbrook Press, 2019.

Rogers, Amy B. *Girls Play Basketball!* New York: PowerKids Press, 2017.

Shea, Therese. *Becoming a Pro Basketball Player*. New York: Gareth Stevens, 2015.

Sylvester, Kevin. *Basketballogy: Supercool Facts You Never Knew*. Toronto, CA: Annick Press, 2017.

Yomtov, Nelson. *Being Your Best at Basketball*. New York: Children's Press, 2017.

Visit 12StoryLibrary.com

Scan the code or use your school's login at **12StoryLibrary.com** for recent updates about this topic and a full digital version of this book. Enjoy free access to:

- Digital ebook
- Breaking news updates
- Live content feeds
- Videos, interactive maps, and graphics
- Additional web resources

Note to educators: Visit 12StoryLibrary.com/register to sign up for free premium website access. Enjoy live content plus a full digital version of every 12-Story Library book you own for every student at your school.

31

Index

All-Star Game, 22

Bryant, Kobe, 16-17, 24-25

charities, 26-27
college basketball, 9, 10, 14-15

daily life, 6-7

high school basketball, 14-15
history, 8-9

injuries, 21
international players, 18-19

James, LeBron, 17, 21, 26

Jordan, Michael, 16

mental stamina, 20
Meyers, Ann, 11
Most Valuable Players (MVP), 22

Naismith, James, 8-9
Naismith Memorial Basketball Hall of Fame, 22-23
National Basketball Association (NBA), 8, 10-11, 14-15, 16, 19, 22, 24
NCAA, 14-15

Olympics, 10

practice, 4, 17, 20

retirement, 22, 24-25, 26
rules, 8-9, 11, 29

salaries, 10, 18, 25
Stoudemire, Amar'e, 19

teamwork, 16-17
travel, 5, 18

Women's Basketball Hall of Fame, 23
Women's National Basketball Association (WNBA), 10-11, 22, 24, 27, 28

youth basketball, 12-13

About the Author
Joanne Mattern has been writing books for children for more than 25 years. She loves to write about sports and has been a basketball fan all her life. Joanne lives in New York State with her family.

READ MORE FROM 12-STORY LIBRARY
Every 12-Story Library Book is available in many fomats. For more information, visit **12StoryLibrary.com**